Bridal Shower Games

Play-Sheets, Instructions & Helpful Tips for the Hostess

CHRONICLE BOOKS

SAN FRANCISCO

Bridal Shower Games
wedding
cakes
bells
rings
a bouquet
presents
Bridal Shower Games
bells
fancy shoe
rings
Bridal

Text © 2007 Chronicle Books LLC
Illustrations © 2007 Maybelle Imasa-Stukuls

ISBN 0-8118-5694-1
Text by *Sharron Wood*
Design by *Kristen Hewitt*
Calligraphy & Illustrations by *Maybelle Imasa-Stukuls*
Typeset in Bodoni
Manufactured in China

Chronicle Books endeavors to use environmentally responsible
paper in its gift and stationery products.

Distributed in Canada by
Raincoast Books
9050 Shaughnessy Street
Vancouver, B.C. V6P 6E5

10 9 8 7 6 5 4 3 2 1

Chronicle Books LLC
680 Second Street
San Francisco, CA 94107
www.chroniclebooks.com

Introduction

Whether a bridal shower is a casual get-together for coworkers or a large affair attended by all of the bride's friends, family, and future in-laws, it should be as unique and special as the guest of honor. Above all, it should be fun—not only for the guests, but for the hostess as well. This is sometimes easier said than done, since in addition to managing the guest list, organizing the decorations, and preparing the food, one must also find creative ways to entertain the guests. But with this game pad in hand, the busy hostess can cross that last item off her list.

Included are eight ready-to-play shower games, you provide the pens. There are fifteen play-sheets included for each game. If you need more sheets, you can easily photocopy extras ahead of time and fill in a sheet of blank stickers for the "Which Famous Couple Are You?" game. Or you can purchase an extra game pad. Choose those that will suit the style of your party and the preferences of the bride and the other guests. You know best whether an icebreaker is in order, or whether the bride and her friends would prefer a trivia competition or a silly game.

The final pages can be used to keep a record of the gifts the bride receives and the name of the gift giver. If you assign a guest sitting next to the bride the job of recording this information, she will surely appreciate having it when she sits down to write her thank-you notes.

Hosting the Games

Which Famous Couple Are You?
Place one game sticker on the back of each player, making sure that they don't see what's written on it. Explain that each sticker has the name of a famous couple printed on it. Each guest will then ask a series of yes or no questions to discover which couple is printed on their sticker. The first person to correctly guess the couple wins.

If I Were the One Getting Married . . .

Have each guest fill in their "If I Were the One Getting Married . . ." game sheet. Collect the sheets and redistribute them randomly. Each guest reads the sheet that has been handed to her, while everyone else tries to guess who filled it out. The player who guesses correctly most consistently is awarded a prize, but the real goal of the game is to break the ice and get everyone acquainted.

How Well Do You Know the Bride?

This game gives everyone a chance to learn a bit more about the guest of honor. After everyone completes the quiz, ask the bride to reveal her answers so the players can tally up their scores, with the highest scorer winning. For an extra bit of fun, have the groom complete the quiz in advance and compare how he did with the guests. Does he know the bride as well as her mother or her best friend?

The Spice of Life

This is the only game that requires a bit of advance preparation. Before the party, collect ten different spice bottles and cover the labels with a strip of paper fastened with tape. Label the bottles 1 through 10 and pass them around for guests to smell and examine (they're not allowed to taste). The guest who identifies the largest number of spices wins. A few key spices that make this game challenging include nutmeg, turmeric, cardamom, fennel, anise, coriander, cumin, cinnamon, allspice, and thyme.

Pearls of Wisdom

This game allows everyone to indulge in a favorite wedding pastime: giving advice to the bride-to-be. The game sheet lists ten topics, from in-laws to children. The guests offer advice, beginning each sentence with either "Always . . ." or "Never. . . ." Expect a lot of silly advice to be mixed in with the sincere. If you like, you can award a prize to the person you think offers the best, or the funniest, advice.

TV Twosomes

This breezy trivia game tests your guests' knowledge of famous romantic pairings from pop culture. Drawing from a roster of modern and classic TV shows, your guests will have three minutes to match the famous TV wife with her mate. If you like, you can divide your

guests into teams to increase the excitement. The answers to this game appear on the inside back cover of this book.

The Animal Dating Game

See whether your guests know their geese from their ganders in this fill-in-the blank test. The players will have two minutes to pair up the list of male animal names with their female counterparts. If you like, you can divide your guests into teams to increase the excitement. The answers to this game appear on the inside back cover of this book.

Honeymoon Trivia

Gauge your guests' knowledge of popular honeymoon destinations with this quiz. Your guests will have three minutes to answer the 13 questions and test their honeymoon IQ. If you like, you can divide your guests into teams to increase the excitement. The answers to this game appear on the inside back cover of this book.

Prizes

Awarding prizes—even inexpensive ones—for winning the games tends to bring out the competitor in everyone. Handmade prizes are almost always sincerely appreciated. If you're known for your almond brittle or mosaic candleholders, by all means bestow them upon the winning guests. Clever packaging elevates the ordinary: Stack cookies and wrap them in colored cellophane, or pack candies in Chinese take-out boxes. If the bride and other guests drink, you can award a bottle of wine or champagne, simply adorned with a bow. Others might prefer specialty loose-leaf teas, which can be packaged with an inexpensive metal mesh tea ball. A small package of fine notepaper or letterpress thank-you cards are both practical and elegant, and little luxuries like fragrant bath soaps, lotions, and scented candles are enjoyed by most women. For glamorous guests, consider shimmery talcum powder, sparkling nail polish, or costume jewelry. When all else fails, gift certificates for a local bookstore or café will do. Whatever your choice of prizes, however, stock up on a few extras, in case any of the games results in a tie.

Bridal
Shower
Games
wedding
bells
rings
cakes
a bouquet
presents
Bridal
Shower
Games
bells
fancy shoe
rings

Which Famous Couple Are You?

Elizabeth Taylor
and
Richard Burton

Annette Bening
and
Warren Beatty

Marge Simpson
and
Homer Simpson

Katharine Hepburn
and
Spencer Tracy

Jackie Kennedy
and
John F. Kennedy

Susan Sarandon
and
Tim Robbins

June Carter Cash
and
Johnny Cash

Grace Kelly
and
Prince Rainier

Which Famous Couple Are You?

Eleanor Roosevelt
and
Franklin D. Roosevelt

Cleopatra
and
Mark Antony

Marilyn Monroe
and
Joe DiMaggio

Lauren Bacall
and
Humphrey Bogart

Lucille Ball
and
Desi Arnaz

Frankenstein
and the
Bride of Frankenstein

Yoko Ono
and
John Lennon

Elizabeth Bennet
and
Fitzwilliam Darcy

If I Were the One Getting Married . . .

*Fill in the blanks in the following sentences, taking care
not to let other people see your answers. When you're done,
hand your answer sheet to the hostess.*

1. After my bachelorette party, everyone would be talking about how I ....
    ....

2. At the wedding I would wear... .

3. In my vows I would promise to...
    ....

4. I would call the wedding off if my husband.................................
    during the wedding.

5. I would serve lots of...at the reception.

6. I would hire... to entertain the guests.

7. I would stock the honeymoon suite with................................. .

8. I would sleep in...on my wedding night.

9. I would travel to...for my honeymoon.

10. I would pack a...in my suitcase.

If I Were the One Getting Married . . .

*Fill in the blanks in the following sentences, taking care
not to let other people see your answers. When you're done,
hand your answer sheet to the hostess.*

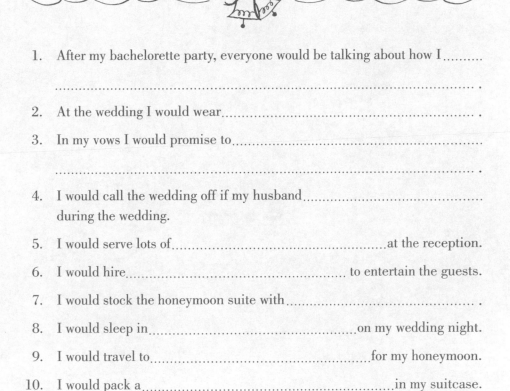

1. After my bachelorette party, everyone would be talking about how I ....

    ....

2. At the wedding I would wear... .

3. In my vows I would promise to...

    ....

4. I would call the wedding off if my husband..
    during the wedding.

5. I would serve lots of..at the reception.

6. I would hire.. to entertain the guests.

7. I would stock the honeymoon suite with.. .

8. I would sleep in..on my wedding night.

9. I would travel to..for my honeymoon.

10. I would pack a..in my suitcase.

If I Were the One Getting Married . . .

*Fill in the blanks in the following sentences, taking care
not to let other people see your answers. When you're done,
hand your answer sheet to the hostess.*

1. After my bachelorette party, everyone would be talking about how I ....
   ....

2. At the wedding I would wear.. .

3. In my vows I would promise to..
   ....

4. I would call the wedding off if my husband...
   during the wedding.

5. I would serve lots of...at the reception.

6. I would hire.. to entertain the guests.

7. I would stock the honeymoon suite with.. .

8. I would sleep in...on my wedding night.

9. I would travel to...for my honeymoon.

10. I would pack a...in my suitcase.

If I Were the One Getting Married . . .

Fill in the blanks in the following sentences, taking care
not to let other people see your answers. When you're done,
hand your answer sheet to the hostess.

1. After my bachelorette party, everyone would be talking about how I ....

   ....

2. At the wedding I would wear ....

3. In my vows I would promise to ....

   ....

4. I would call the wedding off if my husband ....
   during the wedding.

5. I would serve lots of .... at the reception.

6. I would hire .... to entertain the guests.

7. I would stock the honeymoon suite with ....

8. I would sleep in .... on my wedding night.

9. I would travel to .... for my honeymoon.

10. I would pack a .... in my suitcase.

Bridal Shower Games
wedding
bells
rings
cakes
a bouquet
presents
bells
Bridal Shower Games
fancy shoe
rings
Bridal

If I Were the One Getting Married . . .

*Fill in the blanks in the following sentences, taking care
not to let other people see your answers. When you're done,
hand your answer sheet to the hostess.*

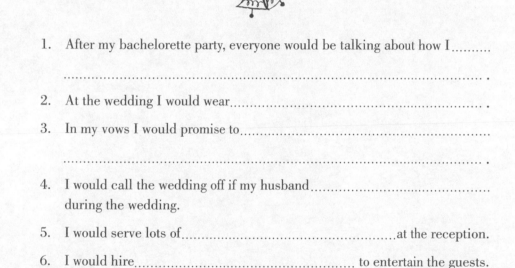

1. After my bachelorette party, everyone would be talking about how I ....
   ....

2. At the wedding I would wear ....

3. In my vows I would promise to ....
   ....

4. I would call the wedding off if my husband ....
   during the wedding.

5. I would serve lots of .... at the reception.

6. I would hire .... to entertain the guests.

7. I would stock the honeymoon suite with ....

8. I would sleep in .... on my wedding night.

9. I would travel to .... for my honeymoon.

10. I would pack a .... in my suitcase.

Bridal Shower Games
wedding
bells
rings
cakes
a bouquet
presents
Bridal Shower Games
bells
No1
fancy shoe
rings
Bridal

If I Were the One Getting Married . . .

*Fill in the blanks in the following sentences, taking care
not to let other people see your answers. When you're done,
hand your answer sheet to the hostess.*

1. After my bachelorette party, everyone would be talking about how I ....
    ....

2. At the wedding I would wear ....

3. In my vows I would promise to ....
    ....

4. I would call the wedding off if my husband ....
    during the wedding.

5. I would serve lots of .... at the reception.

6. I would hire .... to entertain the guests.

7. I would stock the honeymoon suite with ....

8. I would sleep in .... on my wedding night.

9. I would travel to .... for my honeymoon.

10. I would pack a .... in my suitcase.

If I Were the One Getting Married . . .

*Fill in the blanks in the following sentences, taking care
not to let other people see your answers. When you're done,
hand your answer sheet to the hostess.*

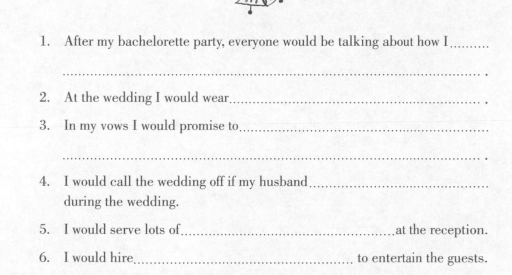

1. After my bachelorette party, everyone would be talking about how I ....

2. At the wedding I would wear ....

3. In my vows I would promise to ....

4. I would call the wedding off if my husband .... during the wedding.

5. I would serve lots of .... at the reception.

6. I would hire .... to entertain the guests.

7. I would stock the honeymoon suite with ....

8. I would sleep in .... on my wedding night.

9. I would travel to .... for my honeymoon.

10. I would pack a .... in my suitcase.

If I Were the One Getting Married . . .

*Fill in the blanks in the following sentences, taking care
not to let other people see your answers. When you're done,
hand your answer sheet to the hostess.*

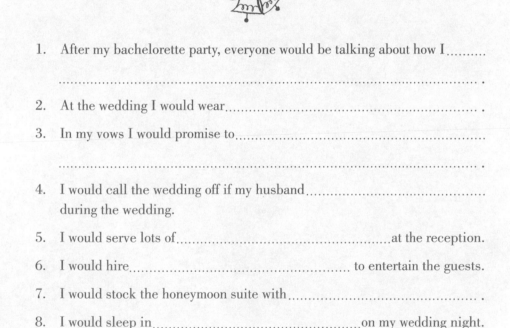

1. After my bachelorette party, everyone would be talking about how I..........

    ....

2. At the wedding I would wear.. .

3. In my vows I would promise to..

    ....

4. I would call the wedding off if my husband.....................................
    during the wedding.

5. I would serve lots of...at the reception.

6. I would hire.................................... to entertain the guests.

7. I would stock the honeymoon suite with........................... .

8. I would sleep in...................................on my wedding night.

9. I would travel to...................................for my honeymoon.

10. I would pack a...................................in my suitcase.

If I Were the One Getting Married . . .

*Fill in the blanks in the following sentences, taking care
not to let other people see your answers. When you're done,
hand your answer sheet to the hostess.*

1. After my bachelorette party, everyone would be talking about how I ....

2. At the wedding I would wear.. .

3. In my vows I would promise to... ....

4. I would call the wedding off if my husband.. during the wedding.

5. I would serve lots of..at the reception.

6. I would hire.. to entertain the guests.

7. I would stock the honeymoon suite with.. .

8. I would sleep in..on my wedding night.

9. I would travel to..for my honeymoon.

10. I would pack a..in my suitcase.

If I Were the One Getting Married . . .

*Fill in the blanks in the following sentences, taking care
not to let other people see your answers. When you're done,
hand your answer sheet to the hostess.*

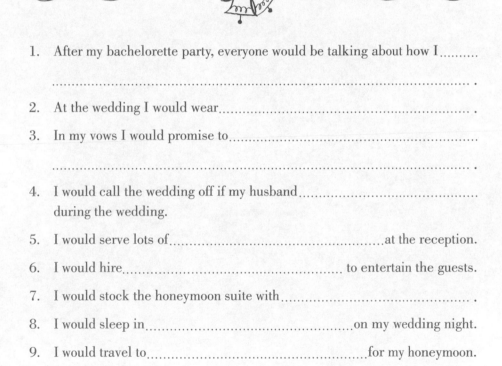

1. After my bachelorette party, everyone would be talking about how I..........
....

2. At the wedding I would wear.. .

3. In my vows I would promise to..
....

4. I would call the wedding off if my husband..
during the wedding.

5. I would serve lots of...at the reception.

6. I would hire.. to entertain the guests.

7. I would stock the honeymoon suite with.. .

8. I would sleep in..on my wedding night.

9. I would travel to..for my honeymoon.

10. I would pack a..in my suitcase.

If I Were the One Getting Married . . .

*Fill in the blanks in the following sentences, taking care
not to let other people see your answers. When you're done,
hand your answer sheet to the hostess.*

1. After my bachelorette party, everyone would be talking about how I ....
    ....

2. At the wedding I would wear.. .

3. In my vows I would promise to..
    ....

4. I would call the wedding off if my husband.................................
    during the wedding.

5. I would serve lots of...at the reception.

6. I would hire.. to entertain the guests.

7. I would stock the honeymoon suite with............................... .

8. I would sleep in...on my wedding night.

9. I would travel to...for my honeymoon.

10. I would pack a...in my suitcase.

If I Were the One Getting Married . . .

*Fill in the blanks in the following sentences, taking care
not to let other people see your answers. When you're done,
hand your answer sheet to the hostess.*

1. After my bachelorette party, everyone would be talking about how I.........
   ....

2. At the wedding I would wear.. .

3. In my vows I would promise to..
   ....

4. I would call the wedding off if my husband..
   during the wedding.

5. I would serve lots of...at the reception.

6. I would hire... to entertain the guests.

7. I would stock the honeymoon suite with.. .

8. I would sleep in...on my wedding night.

9. I would travel to...for my honeymoon.

10. I would pack a...in my suitcase.

If I Were the One Getting Married . . .

*Fill in the blanks in the following sentences, taking care
not to let other people see your answers. When you're done,
hand your answer sheet to the hostess.*

1. After my bachelorette party, everyone would be talking about how I ....

    ....

2. At the wedding I would wear.. .

3. In my vows I would promise to..

    ....

4. I would call the wedding off if my husband.................................
    during the wedding.

5. I would serve lots of...at the reception.

6. I would hire... to entertain the guests.

7. I would stock the honeymoon suite with.................................. .

8. I would sleep in...on my wedding night.

9. I would travel to...for my honeymoon.

10. I would pack a...in my suitcase.

If I Were the One Getting Married . . .

*Fill in the blanks in the following sentences, taking care
not to let other people see your answers. When you're done,
hand your answer sheet to the hostess.*

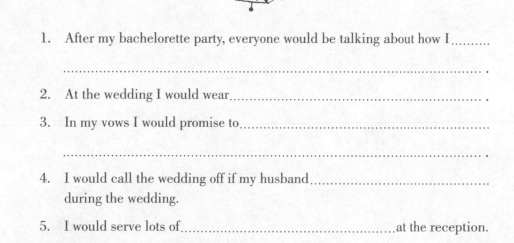

1. After my bachelorette party, everyone would be talking about how I ....

    ....

2. At the wedding I would wear.. .

3. In my vows I would promise to...

    ....

4. I would call the wedding off if my husband.................................
    during the wedding.

5. I would serve lots of..at the reception.

6. I would hire.. to entertain the guests.

7. I would stock the honeymoon suite with.................................... .

8. I would sleep in....................................on my wedding night.

9. I would travel to....................................for my honeymoon.

10. I would pack a....................................in my suitcase.

If I Were the One Getting Married . . .

*Fill in the blanks in the following sentences, taking care
not to let other people see your answers. When you're done,
hand your answer sheet to the hostess.*

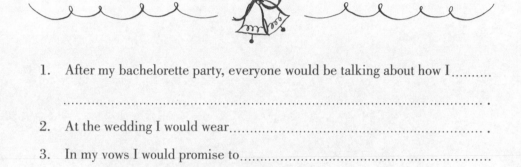

1. After my bachelorette party, everyone would be talking about how I ....
    ....

2. At the wedding I would wear.. .

3. In my vows I would promise to...
    ....

4. I would call the wedding off if my husband...
    during the wedding.

5. I would serve lots of...at the reception.

6. I would hire... to entertain the guests.

7. I would stock the honeymoon suite with... .

8. I would sleep in...on my wedding night.

9. I would travel to...for my honeymoon.

10. I would pack a...in my suitcase.

How Well Do You Know the Bride?

Can you answer the following questions about the guest of honor?

1. What is her mother's middle name? ....

2. What is her middle name? ....

3. What was her major in college? ....

4. What is her favorite drink? ....

5. How did she meet the groom? ....

6. Where did they go on their first date? ....

7. Where was she when she got engaged? ....

8. What does she think is her groom's best physical feature? ....

9. What is her biggest pet peeve about the groom? ....

10. What is the date of her wedding? ....

11. Who is going to be her maid of honor? ....

12. Where is she going on her honeymoon? ....

13. If she could travel anywhere in the world, where would it be? ....
    ....

14. If she were a superhero, who would she be? ....

name   *score*

Bridal Shower Games

presents

bells

wedding cakes

rings

a bouquet

shoe

fancy shoe

How Well Do You Know the Bride?

Can you answer the following questions about the guest of honor?

1. What is her mother's middle name? ....

2. What is her middle name? ....

3. What was her major in college? ....

4. What is her favorite drink? ....

5. How did she meet the groom? ....

6. Where did they go on their first date? ....

7. Where was she when she got engaged? ....

8. What does she think is her groom's best physical feature? ....

9. What is her biggest pet peeve about the groom? ....

10. What is the date of her wedding? ....

11. Who is going to be her maid of honor? ....

12. Where is she going on her honeymoon? ....

13. If she could travel anywhere in the world, where would it be? ....

....

14. If she were a superhero, who would she be? ....

name *score*

How Well Do You Know the Bride?

Can you answer the following questions about the guest of honor?

1. What is her mother's middle name?...

2. What is her middle name?...

3. What was her major in college?..

4. What is her favorite drink?..

5. How did she meet the groom?..

6. Where did they go on their first date?...

7. Where was she when she got engaged?..

8. What does she think is her groom's best physical feature?..........................

9. What is her biggest pet peeve about the groom?......................................

10. What is the date of her wedding?..

11. Who is going to be her maid of honor?..

12. Where is she going on her honeymoon?..

13. If she could travel anywhere in the world, where would it be?.................

....

14. If she were a superhero, who would she be?..

name　　　　　　　　　　　　　　　　　　　　*score*

How Well Do You Know the Bride?

Can you answer the following questions about the guest of honor?

1. What is her mother's middle name? ....

2. What is her middle name? ....

3. What was her major in college? ....

4. What is her favorite drink? ....

5. How did she meet the groom? ....

6. Where did they go on their first date? ....

7. Where was she when she got engaged? ....

8. What does she think is her groom's best physical feature? ....

9. What is her biggest pet peeve about the groom? ....

10. What is the date of her wedding? ....

11. Who is going to be her maid of honor? ....

12. Where is she going on her honeymoon? ....

13. If she could travel anywhere in the world, where would it be? ....
    ....

14. If she were a superhero, who would she be? ....

name   *score*

How Well Do You Know the Bride?

Can you answer the following questions about the guest of honor?

1. What is her mother's middle name? ....
2. What is her middle name? ....
3. What was her major in college? ....
4. What is her favorite drink? ....
5. How did she meet the groom? ....
6. Where did they go on their first date? ....
7. Where was she when she got engaged? ....
8. What does she think is her groom's best physical feature? ....
9. What is her biggest pet peeve about the groom? ....
10. What is the date of her wedding? ....
11. Who is going to be her maid of honor? ....
12. Where is she going on her honeymoon? ....
13. If she could travel anywhere in the world, where would it be? ....
    ....
14. If she were a superhero, who would she be? ....

name   *score*

How Well Do You Know the Bride?

Can you answer the following questions about the guest of honor?

1. What is her mother's middle name? ....
2. What is her middle name? ....
3. What was her major in college? ....
4. What is her favorite drink? ....
5. How did she meet the groom? ....
6. Where did they go on their first date? ....
7. Where was she when she got engaged? ....
8. What does she think is her groom's best physical feature? ....
9. What is her biggest pet peeve about the groom? ....
10. What is the date of her wedding? ....
11. Who is going to be her maid of honor? ....
12. Where is she going on her honeymoon? ....
13. If she could travel anywhere in the world, where would it be? ....
    ....
14. If she were a superhero, who would she be? ....

name *score*

How Well Do You Know the Bride?

Can you answer the following questions about the guest of honor?

1. What is her mother's middle name? ....

2. What is her middle name? ....

3. What was her major in college? ....

4. What is her favorite drink? ....

5. How did she meet the groom? ....

6. Where did they go on their first date? ....

7. Where was she when she got engaged? ....

8. What does she think is her groom's best physical feature? ....

9. What is her biggest pet peeve about the groom? ....

10. What is the date of her wedding? ....

11. Who is going to be her maid of honor? ....

12. Where is she going on her honeymoon? ....

13. If she could travel anywhere in the world, where would it be? ....

    ....

14. If she were a superhero, who would she be? ....

name   *score*

How Well Do You Know the Bride?

Can you answer the following questions about the guest of honor?

1. What is her mother's middle name? ....
2. What is her middle name? ....
3. What was her major in college? ....
4. What is her favorite drink? ....
5. How did she meet the groom? ....
6. Where did they go on their first date? ....
7. Where was she when she got engaged? ....
8. What does she think is her groom's best physical feature? ....
9. What is her biggest pet peeve about the groom? ....
10. What is the date of her wedding? ....
11. Who is going to be her maid of honor? ....
12. Where is she going on her honeymoon? ....
13. If she could travel anywhere in the world, where would it be? ....
    ....
14. If she were a superhero, who would she be? ....

name   *score*

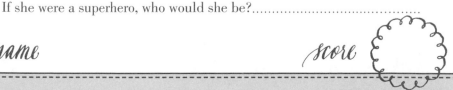

How Well Do You Know the Bride?

Can you answer the following questions about the guest of honor?

1. What is her mother's middle name? ....
2. What is her middle name? ....
3. What was her major in college? ....
4. What is her favorite drink? ....
5. How did she meet the groom? ....
6. Where did they go on their first date? ....
7. Where was she when she got engaged? ....
8. What does she think is her groom's best physical feature? ....
9. What is her biggest pet peeve about the groom? ....
10. What is the date of her wedding? ....
11. Who is going to be her maid of honor? ....
12. Where is she going on her honeymoon? ....
13. If she could travel anywhere in the world, where would it be? ....
    ....
14. If she were a superhero, who would she be? ....

name

score

How Well Do You Know the Bride?

Can you answer the following questions about the guest of honor?

1. What is her mother's middle name? ....
2. What is her middle name? ....
3. What was her major in college? ....
4. What is her favorite drink? ....
5. How did she meet the groom? ....
6. Where did they go on their first date? ....
7. Where was she when she got engaged? ....
8. What does she think is her groom's best physical feature? ....
9. What is her biggest pet peeve about the groom? ....
10. What is the date of her wedding? ....
11. Who is going to be her maid of honor? ....
12. Where is she going on her honeymoon? ....
13. If she could travel anywhere in the world, where would it be? ....
    ....
14. If she were a superhero, who would she be? ....

name   *score*

How Well Do You Know the Bride?

Can you answer the following questions about the guest of honor?

1. What is her mother's middle name? ....
2. What is her middle name? ....
3. What was her major in college? ....
4. What is her favorite drink? ....
5. How did she meet the groom? ....
6. Where did they go on their first date? ....
7. Where was she when she got engaged? ....
8. What does she think is her groom's best physical feature? ....
9. What is her biggest pet peeve about the groom? ....
10. What is the date of her wedding? ....
11. Who is going to be her maid of honor? ....
12. Where is she going on her honeymoon? ....
13. If she could travel anywhere in the world, where would it be? ....
    ....
14. If she were a superhero, who would she be? ....

name   *score*

presents

Bridal
Shower
Games

bells

umbrella

wedding

cakes

rings

shoe

a bouquet

presents

Bridal
Shower
Games

Nº 1

bells

fancy shoe

rings

wedding

cakes

Bridal
Shower

How Well Do You Know the Bride?

Can you answer the following questions about the guest of honor?

1. What is her mother's middle name? ....
2. What is her middle name? ....
3. What was her major in college? ....
4. What is her favorite drink? ....
5. How did she meet the groom? ....
6. Where did they go on their first date? ....
7. Where was she when she got engaged? ....
8. What does she think is her groom's best physical feature? ....
9. What is her biggest pet peeve about the groom? ....
10. What is the date of her wedding? ....
11. Who is going to be her maid of honor? ....
12. Where is she going on her honeymoon? ....
13. If she could travel anywhere in the world, where would it be? ....
    ....
14. If she were a superhero, who would she be? ....

name

score

How Well Do You Know the Bride?

Can you answer the following questions about the guest of honor?

1. What is her mother's middle name? ....

2. What is her middle name? ....

3. What was her major in college? ....

4. What is her favorite drink? ....

5. How did she meet the groom? ....

6. Where did they go on their first date? ....

7. Where was she when she got engaged? ....

8. What does she think is her groom's best physical feature? ....

9. What is her biggest pet peeve about the groom? ....

10. What is the date of her wedding? ....

11. Who is going to be her maid of honor? ....

12. Where is she going on her honeymoon? ....

13. If she could travel anywhere in the world, where would it be? ....
    ....

14. If she were a superhero, who would she be? ....

name   *score*

How Well Do You Know the Bride?

Can you answer the following questions about the guest of honor?

1. What is her mother's middle name? ....
2. What is her middle name? ....
3. What was her major in college? ....
4. What is her favorite drink? ....
5. How did she meet the groom? ....
6. Where did they go on their first date? ....
7. Where was she when she got engaged? ....
8. What does she think is her groom's best physical feature? ....
9. What is her biggest pet peeve about the groom? ....
10. What is the date of her wedding? ....
11. Who is going to be her maid of honor? ....
12. Where is she going on her honeymoon? ....
13. If she could travel anywhere in the world, where would it be? ....
    ....
14. If she were a superhero, who would she be? ....

name

score

How Well Do You Know the Bride?

Can you answer the following questions about the guest of honor?

1. What is her mother's middle name? ....

2. What is her middle name? ....

3. What was her major in college? ....

4. What is her favorite drink? ....

5. How did she meet the groom? ....

6. Where did they go on their first date? ....

7. Where was she when she got engaged? ....

8. What does she think is her groom's best physical feature? ....

9. What is her biggest pet peeve about the groom? ....

10. What is the date of her wedding? ....

11. Who is going to be her maid of honor? ....

12. Where is she going on her honeymoon? ....

13. If she could travel anywhere in the world, where would it be? ....

    ....

14. If she were a superhero, who would she be? ....

name   *score*

The Spice of Life

Each numbered jar contains a different spice or seasoning. Using your senses of sight and smell only, identify each one and write your answer below.

1. ....

2. ....

3. ....

4. ....

5. ....

6. ....

7. ....

8. ....

9. ....

10. ....

name   *score*

The Spice of Life

Each numbered jar contains a different spice or seasoning. Using your senses of sight and smell only, identify each one and write your answer below.

1. ....

2. ....

3. ....

4. ....

5. ....

6. ....

7. ....

8. ....

9. ....

10. ....

name   *score*

The Spice of Life

Each numbered jar contains a different spice or seasoning. Using your senses of sight and smell only, identify each one and write your answer below.

1. ....

2. ....

3. ....

4. ....

5. ....

6. ....

7. ....

8. ....

9. ....

10. ....

name

score

The Spice of Life

Each numbered jar contains a different spice or seasoning. Using your senses of sight and smell only, identify each one and write your answer below.

1. ....

2. ....

3. ....

4. ....

5. ....

6. ....

7. ....

8. ....

9. ....

10. ....

name *score*

The Spice of Life

Each numbered jar contains a different spice or seasoning. Using your senses of sight and smell only, identify each one and write your answer below.

1. ....

2. ....

3. ....

4. ....

5. ....

6. ....

7. ....

8. ....

9. ....

10. ....

name   *score*

The Spice of Life

Each numbered jar contains a different spice or seasoning. Using your senses of sight and smell only, identify each one and write your answer below.

1. ....

2. ....

3. ....

4. ....

5. ....

6. ....

7. ....

8. ....

9. ....

10. ....

name   *score*

The Spice of Life

Each numbered jar contains a different spice or seasoning. Using your senses of sight and smell only, identify each one and write your answer below.

1. ....

2. ....

3. ....

4. ....

5. ....

6. ....

7. ....

8. ....

9. ....

10. ....

name

score

The Spice of Life

Each numbered jar contains a different spice or seasoning. Using your senses of sight and smell only, identify each one and write your answer below.

1. ....

2. ....

3. ....

4. ....

5. ....

6. ....

7. ....

8. ....

9. ....

10. ....

name   *score*

The Spice of Life

Each numbered jar contains a different spice or seasoning. Using your senses of sight and smell only, identify each one and write your answer below.

1. ....

2. ....

3. ....

4. ....

5. ....

6. ....

7. ....

8. ....

9. ....

10. ....

name   *score*

The Spice of Life

Each numbered jar contains a different spice or seasoning. Using your senses of sight and smell only, identify each one and write your answer below.

1. ....

2. ....

3. ....

4. ....

5. ....

6. ....

7. ....

8. ....

9. ....

10. ....

name   *score*

The Spice of Life

Each numbered jar contains a different spice or seasoning. Using your senses of sight and smell only, identify each one and write your answer below.

1. ....

2. ....

3. ....

4. ....

5. ....

6. ....

7. ....

8. ....

9. ....

10. ....

name   *score*

The Spice of Life

Each numbered jar contains a different spice or seasoning. Using your senses of sight and smell only, identify each one and write your answer below.

1. ....

2. ....

3. ....

4. ....

5. ....

6. ....

7. ....

8. ....

9. ....

10. ....

name   *score*

The Spice of Life

Each numbered jar contains a different spice or seasoning. Using your senses of sight and smell only, identify each one and write your answer below.

1. ....

2. ....

3. ....

4. ....

5. ....

6. ....

7. ....

8. ....

9. ....

10. ....

name

score

The Spice of Life

Each numbered jar contains a different spice or seasoning. Using your senses of sight and smell only, identify each one and write your answer below.

1. ....
2. ....
3. ....
4. ....
5. ....
6. ....
7. ....
8. ....
9. ....
10. ....

name   *score*

Bridal Shower Games

bells

wedding

cakes

rings

shoe

a bouquet

presents

Bridal Shower Games

No1

bells

rings

fancy shoe

Bridal Shower

The Spice of Life

Each numbered jar contains a different spice or seasoning. Using your senses of sight and smell only, identify each one and write your answer below.

1. ....

2. ....

3. ....

4. ....

5. ....

6. ....

7. ....

8. ....

9. ....

10. ....

name   *score*

Bridal Shower Games
wedding
bells
rings
cakes
a bouquet
presents
No 1
Bridal Shower Games
bells
fancy shoe
rings

Pearls of Wisdom

Provide your best advice for the bride-to-be on each of the following topics.
Each sentence should start with "Always . . ." or "Never. . . ."

1. The Wedding: ***Always / Never***...
....
....

2. Money: ***Always / Never***..
....
....

3. Honesty: ***Always / Never***..
....
....

4. Old Boyfriends: ***Always / Never***...
....
....

5. Chores: ***Always / Never***...
....
....

6. In-Laws: ***Always / Never***..
....
....

7. Fighting: ***Always / Never***...
....
....

8. Children: ***Always / Never***...
....
....

NAME

Pearls of Wisdom

Provide your best advice for the bride-to-be on each of the following topics.
Each sentence should start with "Always . . ." or "Never. . . ."

1. The Wedding: ***Always / Never***..
....
....

2. Money: ***Always / Never***..
....
....

3. Honesty: ***Always / Never***...
....
....

4. Old Boyfriends: ***Always / Never***...
....
....

5. Chores: ***Always / Never***...
....
....

6. In-Laws: ***Always / Never***...
....
....

7. Fighting: ***Always / Never***...
....
....

8. Children: ***Always / Never***...
....
....

NAME

Pearls of Wisdom

Provide your best advice for the bride-to-be on each of the following topics.
Each sentence should start with "Always . . ." or "Never. . . ."

1. The Wedding: ***Always / Never***..
....
....

2. Money: ***Always / Never***...
....
....

3. Honesty: ***Always / Never***...
....
....

4. Old Boyfriends: ***Always / Never***..
....
....

5. Chores: ***Always / Never***..
....
....

6. In-Laws: ***Always / Never***...
....
....

7. Fighting: ***Always / Never***..
....
....

8. Children: ***Always / Never***..
....
....

NAME

Pearls of Wisdom

Provide your best advice for the bride-to-be on each of the following topics.
Each sentence should start with "Always . . ." or "Never. . . ."

1. The Wedding: **Always / Never**..
....
....

2. Money: **Always / Never**...
....
....

3. Honesty: **Always / Never**...
....
....

4. Old Boyfriends: **Always / Never**...
....
....

5. Chores: **Always / Never**...
....
....

6. In-Laws: **Always / Never**..
....
....

7. Fighting: **Always / Never**...
....
....

8. Children: **Always / Never**...
....
....

name

Pearls of Wisdom

Provide your best advice for the bride-to-be on each of the following topics.
Each sentence should start with "Always . . ." or "Never. . . ."

1. The Wedding: *Always / Never*..
   ....
   ....

2. Money: *Always / Never*...
   ....
   ....

3. Honesty: *Always / Never*...
   ....
   ....

4. Old Boyfriends: *Always / Never*..
   ....
   ....

5. Chores: *Always / Never*...
   ....
   ....

6. In-Laws: *Always / Never*..
   ....
   ....

7. Fighting: *Always / Never*...
   ....
   ....

8. Children: *Always / Never*..
   ....
   ....

NAME

Pearls of Wisdom

Provide your best advice for the bride-to-be on each of the following topics.
Each sentence should start with "Always . . ." or "Never. . . ."

1. The Wedding: ***Always / Never*** ....
   ....
   ....

2. Money: ***Always / Never*** ....
   ....
   ....

3. Honesty: ***Always / Never*** ....
   ....
   ....

4. Old Boyfriends: ***Always / Never*** ....
   ....
   ....

5. Chores: ***Always / Never*** ....
   ....
   ....

6. In-Laws: ***Always / Never*** ....
   ....
   ....

7. Fighting: ***Always / Never*** ....
   ....
   ....

8. Children: ***Always / Never*** ....
   ....
   ....

NAME

Bridal
Shower
Games

bells

wedding

cakes

rings

shoe

a bouquet

presents

Bridal
Shower
Games

bells

fancy shoe

rings

Bridal
Shower

Pearls of Wisdom

Provide your best advice for the bride-to-be on each of the following topics. Each sentence should start with "Always . . ." or "Never. . . ."

1. The Wedding: ***Always / Never***..
....

2. Money: ***Always / Never***...
....

3. Honesty: ***Always / Never***...
....

4. Old Boyfriends: ***Always / Never***..
....

5. Chores: ***Always / Never***..
....

6. In-Laws: ***Always / Never***...
....

7. Fighting: ***Always / Never***..
....

8. Children: ***Always / Never***..
....

NAME

Pearls of Wisdom

Provide your best advice for the bride-to-be on each of the following topics.
Each sentence should start with "Always . . ." or "Never. . . ."

1. The Wedding: *Always / Never*...
   ....
   ....

2. Money: *Always / Never*...
   ....
   ....

3. Honesty: *Always / Never*...
   ....
   ....

4. Old Boyfriends: *Always / Never*...
   ....
   ....

5. Chores: *Always / Never*..
   ....
   ....

6. In-Laws: *Always / Never*...
   ....
   ....

7. Fighting: *Always / Never*..
   ....
   ....

8. Children: *Always / Never*..
   ....
   ....

NAME

Bridal Shower Games
wedding
bells
rings
cakes
a bouquet
presents
Bridal Shower Games
No. 1
bells
fancy shoe
rings

Pearls of Wisdom

Provide your best advice for the bride-to-be on each of the following topics.
Each sentence should start with "Always . . ." or "Never. . . ."

1. The Wedding: *Always / Never*..
....
....

2. Money: *Always / Never*..
....
....

3. Honesty: *Always / Never*..
....
....

4. Old Boyfriends: *Always / Never*..
....
....

5. Chores: *Always / Never*..
....
....

6. In-Laws: *Always / Never*...
....
....

7. Fighting: *Always / Never*..
....
....

8. Children: *Always / Never*..
....
....

NAME

Pearls of Wisdom

Provide your best advice for the bride-to-be on each of the following topics.
Each sentence should start with "Always . . ." or "Never. . . ."

1. The Wedding: ***Always / Never***..
    ....

2. Money: ***Always / Never***..
    ....

3. Honesty: ***Always / Never***..
    ....

4. Old Boyfriends: ***Always / Never***..
    ....

5. Chores: ***Always / Never***..
    ....

6. In-Laws: ***Always / Never***..
    ....

7. Fighting: ***Always / Never***..
    ....

8. Children: ***Always / Never***..
    ....

NAME

presents

Bridal Shower Games

bells

wedding

rings

cakes

a bouquet

shoe

presents

Bridal Shower Games

bells

No 1

wedding

rings

fancy shoe

Bridal Shower

Pearls of Wisdom

Provide your best advice for the bride-to-be on each of the following topics. Each sentence should start with "Always . . ." or "Never. . . ."

1. The Wedding: ***Always / Never***...
....

2. Money: ***Always / Never***..
....

3. Honesty: ***Always / Never***...
....

4. Old Boyfriends: ***Always / Never***..
....

5. Chores: ***Always / Never***...
....

6. In-Laws: ***Always / Never***..
....

7. Fighting: ***Always / Never***...
....

8. Children: ***Always / Never***...
....

NAME

Pearls of Wisdom

Provide your best advice for the bride-to-be on each of the following topics.
Each sentence should start with "Always . . ." or "Never. . . ."

1. The Wedding: ***Always / Never***..
   ....
   ....

2. Money: ***Always / Never***...
   ....
   ....

3. Honesty: ***Always / Never***...
   ....
   ....

4. Old Boyfriends: ***Always / Never***..
   ....
   ....

5. Chores: ***Always / Never***..
   ....
   ....

6. In-Laws: ***Always / Never***..
   ....
   ....

7. Fighting: ***Always / Never***...
   ....
   ....

8. Children: ***Always / Never***...
   ....
   ....

NAME

Pearls of Wisdom

Provide your best advice for the bride-to-be on each of the following topics.
Each sentence should start with "Always . . ." or "Never. . . ."

1. The Wedding: ***Always / Never*** ....
    ....

2. Money: ***Always / Never*** ....
    ....

3. Honesty: ***Always / Never*** ....
    ....

4. Old Boyfriends: ***Always / Never*** ....
    ....

5. Chores: ***Always / Never*** ....
    ....

6. In-Laws: ***Always / Never*** ....
    ....

7. Fighting: ***Always / Never*** ....
    ....

8. Children: ***Always / Never*** ....
    ....

name

Pearls of Wisdom

Provide your best advice for the bride-to-be on each of the following topics.
Each sentence should start with "Always . . ." or "Never. . . ."

1. The Wedding: ***Always / Never*** ....
....
....

2. Money: ***Always / Never*** ....
....
....

3. Honesty: ***Always / Never*** ....
....
....

4. Old Boyfriends: ***Always / Never*** ....
....
....

5. Chores: ***Always / Never*** ....
....
....

6. In-Laws: ***Always / Never*** ....
....
....

7. Fighting: ***Always / Never*** ....
....
....

8. Children: ***Always / Never*** ....
....
....

NAME

Pearls of Wisdom

Provide your best advice for the bride-to-be on each of the following topics.
Each sentence should start with "Always . . ." or "Never. . . ."

1. The Wedding: ***Always / Never***...
   ....

2. Money: ***Always / Never***...
   ....

3. Honesty: ***Always / Never***...
   ....

4. Old Boyfriends: ***Always / Never***...
   ....

5. Chores: ***Always / Never***..
   ....

6. In-Laws: ***Always / Never***...
   ....

7. Fighting: ***Always / Never***..
   ....

8. Children: ***Always / Never***..
   ....

name

TV Twosomes

For each of the famous TV wives listed below, write the name of her TV husband and the show on which they appeared. Each answer is worth one point. You have three minutes to finish.

	Wife	Husband	TV Show
1.	June Cleaver	....	....
2.	Marge Simpson	....	....
3.	Clair Huxtable	....	....
4.	Laura Spencer	....	....
5.	Elyse Keaton	....	....
6.	Carol Brady	....	....
7.	Morticia Addams	....	....
8.	Kirsten Cohen	....	....
9.	Marion Cunningham	....	....
10.	Caroline Ingalls	....	....
11.	Edith Bunker	....	....
12.	Laura Petrie	....	....
13.	Monica Geller Bing	....	....
14.	Jill Taylor	....	....
15.	Eunice Wentworth Howell	....	....
16.	Lynette Scavo	....	....

name   *score*

Bridal
Shower
Games

bells

wedding

cakes

rings

a bouquet

presents

Bridal
Shower
Games

bells

N°1

rings

fancy shoe

Bridal
Shower

TV Twosomes

For each of the famous TV wives listed below, write the name of her TV husband and the show on which they appeared. Each answer is worth one point. You have three minutes to finish.

	Wife	Husband	TV Show
1.	June Cleaver		
2.	Marge Simpson		
3.	Clair Huxtable		
4.	Laura Spencer		
5.	Elyse Keaton		
6.	Carol Brady		
7.	Morticia Addams		
8.	Kirsten Cohen		
9.	Marion Cunningham		
10.	Caroline Ingalls		
11.	Edith Bunker		
12.	Laura Petrie		
13.	Monica Geller Bing		
14.	Jill Taylor		
15.	Eunice Wentworth Howell		
16.	Lynette Scavo		

NAME

score

TV Twosomes

For each of the famous TV wives listed below, write the name of her TV husband and the show on which they appeared. Each answer is worth one point. You have three minutes to finish.

	Wife	Husband	TV Show
1.	June Cleaver	....	....
2.	Marge Simpson	....	....
3.	Clair Huxtable	....	....
4.	Laura Spencer	....	....
5.	Elyse Keaton	....	....
6.	Carol Brady	....	....
7.	Morticia Addams	....	....
8.	Kirsten Cohen	....	....
9.	Marion Cunningham	....	....
10.	Caroline Ingalls	....	....
11.	Edith Bunker	....	....
12.	Laura Petrie	....	....
13.	Monica Geller Bing	....	....
14.	Jill Taylor	....	....
15.	Eunice Wentworth Howell	....	....
16.	Lynette Scavo	....	....

name   *score*

TV Twosomes

For each of the famous TV wives listed below, write the name of her TV husband and the show on which they appeared. Each answer is worth one point. You have three minutes to finish.

	Wife	Husband	TV Show
1.	June Cleaver		
2.	Marge Simpson		
3.	Clair Huxtable		
4.	Laura Spencer		
5.	Elyse Keaton		
6.	Carol Brady		
7.	Morticia Addams		
8.	Kirsten Cohen		
9.	Marion Cunningham		
10.	Caroline Ingalls		
11.	Edith Bunker		
12.	Laura Petrie		
13.	Monica Geller Bing		
14.	Jill Taylor		
15.	Eunice Wentworth Howell		
16.	Lynette Scavo		

name

score

TV Twosomes

For each of the famous TV wives listed below, write the name of her TV husband and the show on which they appeared. Each answer is worth one point. You have three minutes to finish.

	Wife	Husband	TV Show
1.	June Cleaver		
2.	Marge Simpson		
3.	Clair Huxtable		
4.	Laura Spencer		
5.	Elyse Keaton		
6.	Carol Brady		
7.	Morticia Addams		
8.	Kirsten Cohen		
9.	Marion Cunningham		
10.	Caroline Ingalls		
11.	Edith Bunker		
12.	Laura Petrie		
13.	Monica Geller Bing		
14.	Jill Taylor		
15.	Eunice Wentworth Howell		
16.	Lynette Scavo		

name   *score*

TV Twosomes

For each of the famous TV wives listed below, write the name of her TV husband and the show on which they appeared. Each answer is worth one point. You have three minutes to finish.

	Wife	Husband	TV Show
1.	June Cleaver		
2.	Marge Simpson		
3.	Clair Huxtable		
4.	Laura Spencer		
5.	Elyse Keaton		
6.	Carol Brady		
7.	Morticia Addams		
8.	Kirsten Cohen		
9.	Marion Cunningham		
10.	Caroline Ingalls		
11.	Edith Bunker		
12.	Laura Petrie		
13.	Monica Geller Bing		
14.	Jill Taylor		
15.	Eunice Wentworth Howell		
16.	Lynette Scavo		

name

score

TV Twosomes

For each of the famous TV wives listed below, write the name of her TV husband and the show on which they appeared. Each answer is worth one point. You have three minutes to finish.

	Wife	Husband	TV Show
1.	June Cleaver	....	....
2.	Marge Simpson	....	....
3.	Clair Huxtable	....	....
4.	Laura Spencer	....	....
5.	Elyse Keaton	....	....
6.	Carol Brady	....	....
7.	Morticia Addams	....	....
8.	Kirsten Cohen	....	....
9.	Marion Cunningham	....	....
10.	Caroline Ingalls	....	....
11.	Edith Bunker	....	....
12.	Laura Petrie	....	....
13.	Monica Geller Bing	....	....
14.	Jill Taylor	....	....
15.	Eunice Wentworth Howell	....	....
16.	Lynette Scavo	....	....

name   *score*

TV Twosomes

For each of the famous TV wives listed below, write the name of her TV husband and the show on which they appeared. Each answer is worth one point. You have three minutes to finish.

	Wife	Husband	TV Show
1.	June Cleaver		
2.	Marge Simpson		
3.	Clair Huxtable		
4.	Laura Spencer		
5.	Elyse Keaton		
6.	Carol Brady		
7.	Morticia Addams		
8.	Kirsten Cohen		
9.	Marion Cunningham		
10.	Caroline Ingalls		
11.	Edith Bunker		
12.	Laura Petrie		
13.	Monica Geller Bing		
14.	Jill Taylor		
15.	Eunice Wentworth Howell		
16.	Lynette Scavo		

name *score*

TV Twosomes

For each of the famous TV wives listed below, write the name of her TV husband and the show on which they appeared. Each answer is worth one point. You have three minutes to finish.

	Wife	*Husband*	*TV Show*
1.	June Cleaver		
2.	Marge Simpson		
3.	Clair Huxtable		
4.	Laura Spencer		
5.	Elyse Keaton		
6.	Carol Brady		
7.	Morticia Addams		
8.	Kirsten Cohen		
9.	Marion Cunningham		
10.	Caroline Ingalls		
11.	Edith Bunker		
12.	Laura Petrie		
13.	Monica Geller Bing		
14.	Jill Taylor		
15.	Eunice Wentworth Howell		
16.	Lynette Scavo		

name

score

Bridal Shower Games
wedding
bells
rings
cakes
a bouquet
presents
No 1
bells
fancy shoe
rings
Bridal Shower

TV Twosomes

For each of the famous TV wives listed below, write the name of her TV husband and the show on which they appeared. Each answer is worth one point. You have three minutes to finish.

Wife	Husband	TV Show
1. June Cleaver		
2. Marge Simpson		
3. Clair Huxtable		
4. Laura Spencer		
5. Elyse Keaton		
6. Carol Brady		
7. Morticia Addams		
8. Kirsten Cohen		
9. Marion Cunningham		
10. Caroline Ingalls		
11. Edith Bunker		
12. Laura Petrie		
13. Monica Geller Bing		
14. Jill Taylor		
15. Eunice Wentworth Howell		
16. Lynette Scavo		

name

score

TV Twosomes

For each of the famous TV wives listed below, write the name of her TV husband and the show on which they appeared. Each answer is worth one point. You have three minutes to finish.

	Wife	*Husband*	*TV Show*
1.	June Cleaver	....	....
2.	Marge Simpson	....	....
3.	Clair Huxtable	....	....
4.	Laura Spencer	....	....
5.	Elyse Keaton	....	....
6.	Carol Brady	....	....
7.	Morticia Addams	....	....
8.	Kirsten Cohen	....	....
9.	Marion Cunningham	....	....
10.	Caroline Ingalls	....	....
11.	Edith Bunker	....	....
12.	Laura Petrie	....	....
13.	Monica Geller Bing	....	....
14.	Jill Taylor	....	....
15.	Eunice Wentworth Howell	....	....
16.	Lynette Scavo	....	....

name

score

TV Twosomes

For each of the famous TV wives listed below, write the name of her TV
husband and the show on which they appeared. Each answer is worth one point.
You have three minutes to finish.

	Wife	Husband	TV Show
1.	June Cleaver	....	....
2.	Marge Simpson	....	....
3.	Clair Huxtable	....	....
4.	Laura Spencer	....	....
5.	Elyse Keaton	....	....
6.	Carol Brady	....	....
7.	Morticia Addams	....	....
8.	Kirsten Cohen	....	....
9.	Marion Cunningham	....	....
10.	Caroline Ingalls	....	....
11.	Edith Bunker	....	....
12.	Laura Petrie	....	....
13.	Monica Geller Bing	....	....
14.	Jill Taylor	....	....
15.	Eunice Wentworth Howell	....	....
16.	Lynette Scavo	....	....

name   *score*

TV Twosomes

For each of the famous TV wives listed below, write the name of her TV husband and the show on which they appeared. Each answer is worth one point. You have three minutes to finish.

	Wife	Husband	TV Show
1.	June Cleaver	....	....
2.	Marge Simpson	....	....
3.	Clair Huxtable	....	....
4.	Laura Spencer	....	....
5.	Elyse Keaton	....	....
6.	Carol Brady	....	....
7.	Morticia Addams	....	....
8.	Kirsten Cohen	....	....
9.	Marion Cunningham	....	....
10.	Caroline Ingalls	....	....
11.	Edith Bunker	....	....
12.	Laura Petrie	....	....
13.	Monica Geller Bing	....	....
14.	Jill Taylor	....	....
15.	Eunice Wentworth Howell	....	....
16.	Lynette Scavo	....	....

name

score

TV Twosomes

For each of the famous TV wives listed below, write the name of her TV husband and the show on which they appeared. Each answer is worth one point. You have three minutes to finish.

	Wife	Husband	TV Show
1.	June Cleaver	....	....
2.	Marge Simpson	....	....
3.	Clair Huxtable	....	....
4.	Laura Spencer	....	....
5.	Elyse Keaton	....	....
6.	Carol Brady	....	....
7.	Morticia Addams	....	....
8.	Kirsten Cohen	....	....
9.	Marion Cunningham	....	....
10.	Caroline Ingalls	....	....
11.	Edith Bunker	....	....
12.	Laura Petrie	....	....
13.	Monica Geller Bing	....	....
14.	Jill Taylor	....	....
15.	Eunice Wentworth Howell	....	....
16.	Lynette Scavo	....	....

name

score

TV Twosomes

For each of the famous TV wives listed below, write the name of her TV husband and the show on which they appeared. Each answer is worth one point. You have three minutes to finish.

	Wife	Husband	TV Show
1.	June Cleaver	....	....
2.	Marge Simpson	....	....
3.	Clair Huxtable	....	....
4.	Laura Spencer	....	....
5.	Elyse Keaton	....	....
6.	Carol Brady	....	....
7.	Morticia Addams	....	....
8.	Kirsten Cohen	....	....
9.	Marion Cunningham	....	....
10.	Caroline Ingalls	....	....
11.	Edith Bunker	....	....
12.	Laura Petrie	....	....
13.	Monica Geller Bing	....	....
14.	Jill Taylor	....	....
15.	Eunice Wentworth Howell	....	....
16.	Lynette Scavo	....	....

name   *score*

The Animal Dating Game

For each of the following animals, identify the male's female counterpart.
You have two minutes to complete.

	Animal	Male	Female
1.	Horse	Stallion	....
2.	Elephant	Bull	....
3.	Chicken	Rooster	....
4.	Swan	Cob	....
5.	Deer	Buck	....
6.	Kangaroo	Boomer or Jack	....
7.	Swine	Boar	....
8.	Goat	Billy	....
9.	Donkey	Jack	....
10.	Sheep	Ram	....
11.	Fox	Reynard	....

name

score

The Animal Dating Game

*For each of the following animals, identify the male's female counterpart.
You have two minutes to complete.*

	Animal	Male	Female
1.	Horse	Stallion	....
2.	Elephant	Bull	....
3.	Chicken	Rooster	....
4.	Swan	Cob	....
5.	Deer	Buck	....
6.	Kangaroo	Boomer or Jack	....
7.	Swine	Boar	....
8.	Goat	Billy	....
9.	Donkey	Jack	....
10.	Sheep	Ram	....
11.	Fox	Reynard	....

Name

score

The Animal Dating Game

For each of the following animals, identify the male's female counterpart.
You have two minutes to complete.

	Animal	Male	Female
1.	Horse	Stallion	....
2.	Elephant	Bull	....
3.	Chicken	Rooster	....
4.	Swan	Cob	....
5.	Deer	Buck	....
6.	Kangaroo	Boomer or Jack	....
7.	Swine	Boar	....
8.	Goat	Billy	....
9.	Donkey	Jack	....
10.	Sheep	Ram	....
11.	Fox	Reynard	....

name

score

Bridal Shower Games
wedding
bells
rings
cakes
a bouquet
presents
Bridal Shower Games
bells
fancy shoe
rings
Bridal Shower

The Animal Dating Game

For each of the following animals, identify the male's female counterpart.
You have two minutes to complete.

Animal	Male	Female
1. Horse	Stallion	....
2. Elephant	Bull	....
3. Chicken	Rooster	....
4. Swan	Cob	....
5. Deer	Buck	....
6. Kangaroo	Boomer or Jack	....
7. Swine	Boar	....
8. Goat	Billy	....
9. Donkey	Jack	....
10. Sheep	Ram	....
11. Fox	Reynard	....

The Animal Dating Game

For each of the following animals, identify the male's female counterpart.
You have two minutes to complete.

	Animal	Male	Female
1.	Horse	Stallion	....
2.	Elephant	Bull	....
3.	Chicken	Rooster	....
4.	Swan	Cob	....
5.	Deer	Buck	....
6.	Kangaroo	Boomer or Jack	....
7.	Swine	Boar	....
8.	Goat	Billy	....
9.	Donkey	Jack	....
10.	Sheep	Ram	....
11.	Fox	Reynard	....

name   *score*

The Animal Dating Game

For each of the following animals, identify the male's female counterpart.
You have two minutes to complete.

	Animal	Male	Female
1.	Horse	Stallion	....
2.	Elephant	Bull	....
3.	Chicken	Rooster	....
4.	Swan	Cob	....
5.	Deer	Buck	....
6.	Kangaroo	Boomer or Jack	....
7.	Swine	Boar	....
8.	Goat	Billy	....
9.	Donkey	Jack	....
10.	Sheep	Ram	....
11.	Fox	Reynard	....

name   *score*

The Animal Dating Game

For each of the following animals, identify the male's female counterpart.
You have two minutes to complete.

	Animal	Male	Female
1.	Horse	Stallion	....
2.	Elephant	Bull	....
3.	Chicken	Rooster	....
4.	Swan	Cob	....
5.	Deer	Buck	....
6.	Kangaroo	Boomer or Jack	....
7.	Swine	Boar	....
8.	Goat	Billy	....
9.	Donkey	Jack	....
10.	Sheep	Ram	....
11.	Fox	Reynard	....

name   *score*

The Animal Dating Game

For each of the following animals, identify the male's female counterpart.
You have two minutes to complete.

	Animal	Male	Female
1.	Horse	Stallion	....
2.	Elephant	Bull	....
3.	Chicken	Rooster	....
4.	Swan	Cob	....
5.	Deer	Buck	....
6.	Kangaroo	Boomer or Jack	....
7.	Swine	Boar	....
8.	Goat	Billy	....
9.	Donkey	Jack	....
10.	Sheep	Ram	....
11.	Fox	Reynard	....

name   *score*

The Animal Dating Game

For each of the following animals, identify the male's female counterpart.
You have two minutes to complete.

	Animal	Male	Female
1.	Horse	Stallion	....
2.	Elephant	Bull	....
3.	Chicken	Rooster	....
4.	Swan	Cob	....
5.	Deer	Buck	....
6.	Kangaroo	Boomer or Jack	....
7.	Swine	Boar	....
8.	Goat	Billy	....
9.	Donkey	Jack	....
10.	Sheep	Ram	....
11.	Fox	Reynard	....

name

score

Bridal Shower Games

bells

wedding cakes

rings

a bouquet

presents

Bridal Shower Games

fancy shoe

rings

Bridal Shower

The Animal Dating Game

For each of the following animals, identify the male's female counterpart.
You have two minutes to complete.

	Animal	Male	Female
1.	Horse	Stallion	....
2.	Elephant	Bull	....
3.	Chicken	Rooster	....
4.	Swan	Cob	....
5.	Deer	Buck	....
6.	Kangaroo	Boomer or Jack	....
7.	Swine	Boar	....
8.	Goat	Billy	....
9.	Donkey	Jack	....
10.	Sheep	Ram	....
11.	Fox	Reynard	....

name

score

The Animal Dating Game

For each of the following animals, identify the male's female counterpart.
You have two minutes to complete.

	Animal	Male	Female
1.	Horse	Stallion	....
2.	Elephant	Bull	....
3.	Chicken	Rooster	....
4.	Swan	Cob	....
5.	Deer	Buck	....
6.	Kangaroo	Boomer or Jack	....
7.	Swine	Boar	....
8.	Goat	Billy	....
9.	Donkey	Jack	....
10.	Sheep	Ram	....
11.	Fox	Reynard	....

name *score*

Bridal
Shower
Games
wedding
bells
rings
cakes
a bouquet
presents
Bridal
Shower
Games
No. 1
bells
fancy shoe
rings
Bridal
Shower

The Animal Dating Game

For each of the following animals, identify the male's female counterpart.
You have two minutes to complete.

	Animal	Male	Female
1.	Horse	Stallion	....
2.	Elephant	Bull	....
3.	Chicken	Rooster	....
4.	Swan	Cob	....
5.	Deer	Buck	....
6.	Kangaroo	Boomer or Jack	....
7.	Swine	Boar	....
8.	Goat	Billy	....
9.	Donkey	Jack	....
10.	Sheep	Ram	....
11.	Fox	Reynard	....

Bridal
Shower
Games
wedding
bells
rings
cakes
shoe
a bouquet
presents
Bridal
Shower
Games
No 1
bells
fancy shoe
rings
Bridal
Shower

The Animal Dating Game

For each of the following animals, identify the male's female counterpart.
You have two minutes to complete.

	Animal	Male	Female
1.	Horse	Stallion	....
2.	Elephant	Bull	....
3.	Chicken	Rooster	....
4.	Swan	Cob	....
5.	Deer	Buck	....
6.	Kangaroo	Boomer or Jack	....
7.	Swine	Boar	....
8.	Goat	Billy	....
9.	Donkey	Jack	....
10.	Sheep	Ram	....
11.	Fox	Reynard	....

name   *score*

The Animal Dating Game

For each of the following animals, identify the male's female counterpart.
You have two minutes to complete.

	Animal	Male	Female
1.	Horse	Stallion	....
2.	Elephant	Bull	....
3.	Chicken	Rooster	....
4.	Swan	Cob	....
5.	Deer	Buck	....
6.	Kangaroo	Boomer or Jack	....
7.	Swine	Boar	....
8.	Goat	Billy	....
9.	Donkey	Jack	....
10.	Sheep	Ram	....
11.	Fox	Reynard	....

name

score

Bridal Shower Games
wedding
bells
rings
cakes
a bouquet
presents
Bridal Shower Games
bells
fancy shoe
rings

The Animal Dating Game

For each of the following animals, identify the male's female counterpart.
You have two minutes to complete.

	Animal	Male	Female
1.	Horse	Stallion	....
2.	Elephant	Bull	....
3.	Chicken	Rooster	....
4.	Swan	Cob	....
5.	Deer	Buck	....
6.	Kangaroo	Boomer or Jack	....
7.	Swine	Boar	....
8.	Goat	Billy	....
9.	Donkey	Jack	....
10.	Sheep	Ram	....
11.	Fox	Reynard	....

name   *score*

Honeymoon Trivia

How much do you know about some of the most popular honeymoon destinations? You have three minutes to finish.

1. What romantic city is known as the City of Light? ....

2. What popular honeymoon destination is the largest island in French Polynesia?
....

3. In Bermuda, what is customarily placed on top of the wedding cake? ....
....

4. Which state in the U.S. is the most popular destination for honeymooners? ....

5. A study by UNESCO once concluded that 40 percent of the world's historic and artistic assets are in which country? ....

6. In Jamaica, wedding cakes are typically made with dried fruits that have been soaked in what? ....

7. In which country might you find a heart-shaped piñata at a wedding? ....

8. What might a bride in Greece tuck into her glove to ensure a sweet life? ....
....

9. Those with a taste for extravagance can get married at Las Vegas Villa, former home of what famous flamboyant performer? ....

10. This city, one of the most popular honeymoon destinations in the U.S., is a sister city to the equally romantic Assisi, Italy; Paris, France; and Sydney, Australia.
....

11. What popular honeymoon destination straddles the U.S.-Canadian border?
....

12. In which romantic city are civil marriages performed in the Palazzo Cavalli, a 16th-century castle overlooking the Grand Canal? ....

name   *score*

Honeymoon Trivia

How much do you know about some of the most popular honeymoon destinations? You have three minutes to finish.

1. What romantic city is known as the City of Light? ....

2. What popular honeymoon destination is the largest island in French Polynesia?
   ....

3. In Bermuda, what is customarily placed on top of the wedding cake?.........................
   ....

4. Which state in the U.S. is the most popular destination for honeymooners?.................

5. A study by UNESCO once concluded that 40 percent of the world's historic and artistic assets are in which country?...

6. In Jamaica, wedding cakes are typically made with dried fruits that have been soaked in what?..

7. In which country might you find a heart-shaped piñata at a wedding?.........................

8. What might a bride in Greece tuck into her glove to ensure a sweet life?....................
   ....

9. Those with a taste for extravagance can get married at Las Vegas Villa, former home of what famous flamboyant performer? ....

10. This city, one of the most popular honeymoon destinations in the U.S., is a sister city to the equally romantic Assisi, Italy; Paris, France; and Sydney, Australia.
    ....

11. What popular honeymoon destination straddles the U.S.-Canadian border?
    ....

12. In which romantic city are civil marriages performed in the Palazzo Cavalli, a 16th-century castle overlooking the Grand Canal?.............................

name   *score*

Honeymoon Trivia

How much do you know about some of the most popular honeymoon destinations? You have three minutes to finish.

1. What romantic city is known as the City of Light? ....

2. What popular honeymoon destination is the largest island in French Polynesia?
....

3. In Bermuda, what is customarily placed on top of the wedding cake? ....
....

4. Which state in the U.S. is the most popular destination for honeymooners? ....

5. A study by UNESCO once concluded that 40 percent of the world's historic and artistic assets are in which country? ....

6. In Jamaica, wedding cakes are typically made with dried fruits that have been soaked in what? ....

7. In which country might you find a heart-shaped piñata at a wedding? ....

8. What might a bride in Greece tuck into her glove to ensure a sweet life? ....
....

9. Those with a taste for extravagance can get married at Las Vegas Villa, former home of what famous flamboyant performer? ....

10. This city, one of the most popular honeymoon destinations in the U.S., is a sister city to the equally romantic Assisi, Italy; Paris, France; and Sydney, Australia.
....

11. What popular honeymoon destination straddles the U.S.-Canadian border?
....

12. In which romantic city are civil marriages performed in the Palazzo Cavalli, a 16th-century castle overlooking the Grand Canal? ....

name   *score*

Honeymoon Trivia

How much do you know about some of the most popular honeymoon destinations? You have three minutes to finish.

1. What romantic city is known as the City of Light? ....

2. What popular honeymoon destination is the largest island in French Polynesia?
   ....

3. In Bermuda, what is customarily placed on top of the wedding cake? ....
   ....

4. Which state in the U.S. is the most popular destination for honeymooners? ....

5. A study by UNESCO once concluded that 40 percent of the world's historic and artistic assets are in which country? ....

6. In Jamaica, wedding cakes are typically made with dried fruits that have been soaked in what? ....

7. In which country might you find a heart-shaped piñata at a wedding? ....

8. What might a bride in Greece tuck into her glove to ensure a sweet life? ....
   ....

9. Those with a taste for extravagance can get married at Las Vegas Villa, former home of what famous flamboyant performer? ....

10. This city, one of the most popular honeymoon destinations in the U.S., is a sister city to the equally romantic Assisi, Italy; Paris, France; and Sydney, Australia.
    ....

11. What popular honeymoon destination straddles the U.S.-Canadian border?
    ....

12. In which romantic city are civil marriages performed in the Palazzo Cavalli, a 16th-century castle overlooking the Grand Canal? ....

name   *score*

Honeymoon Trivia

How much do you know about some of the most popular honeymoon destinations? You have three minutes to finish.

1. What romantic city is known as the City of Light? ....

2. What popular honeymoon destination is the largest island in French Polynesia?
   ....

3. In Bermuda, what is customarily placed on top of the wedding cake? ....
   ....

4. Which state in the U.S. is the most popular destination for honeymooners? ....

5. A study by UNESCO once concluded that 40 percent of the world's historic and artistic assets are in which country? ....

6. In Jamaica, wedding cakes are typically made with dried fruits that have been soaked in what? ....

7. In which country might you find a heart-shaped piñata at a wedding? ....

8. What might a bride in Greece tuck into her glove to ensure a sweet life? ....
   ....

9. Those with a taste for extravagance can get married at Las Vegas Villa, former home of what famous flamboyant performer? ....

10. This city, one of the most popular honeymoon destinations in the U.S., is a sister city to the equally romantic Assisi, Italy; Paris, France; and Sydney, Australia.
    ....

11. What popular honeymoon destination straddles the U.S.-Canadian border?
    ....

12. In which romantic city are civil marriages performed in the Palazzo Cavalli, a 16th-century castle overlooking the Grand Canal? ....

name   *score*

Honeymoon Trivia

How much do you know about some of the most popular honeymoon destinations? You have three minutes to finish.

1. What romantic city is known as the City of Light? ....

2. What popular honeymoon destination is the largest island in French Polynesia?
....

3. In Bermuda, what is customarily placed on top of the wedding cake? ....
....

4. Which state in the U.S. is the most popular destination for honeymooners? ....

5. A study by UNESCO once concluded that 40 percent of the world's historic and artistic assets are in which country? ....

6. In Jamaica, wedding cakes are typically made with dried fruits that have been soaked in what? ....

7. In which country might you find a heart-shaped piñata at a wedding? ....

8. What might a bride in Greece tuck into her glove to ensure a sweet life? ....
....

9. Those with a taste for extravagance can get married at Las Vegas Villa, former home of what famous flamboyant performer? ....

10. This city, one of the most popular honeymoon destinations in the U.S., is a sister city to the equally romantic Assisi, Italy; Paris, France; and Sydney, Australia.
....

11. What popular honeymoon destination straddles the U.S.-Canadian border?
....

12. In which romantic city are civil marriages performed in the Palazzo Cavalli, a 16th-century castle overlooking the Grand Canal? ....

name　　　　　　　　　　　　　　　　　　　　*score*

Bridal Shower Games

bells

wedding
cakes

rings

shoe

a bouquet

presents

Bridal Shower Games

bells

wedding

rings

fancy shoe

Bridal Shower

Honeymoon Trivia

How much do you know about some of the most popular honeymoon destinations? You have three minutes to finish.

1. What romantic city is known as the City of Light? ....

2. What popular honeymoon destination is the largest island in French Polynesia?
....

3. In Bermuda, what is customarily placed on top of the wedding cake? ....
....

4. Which state in the U.S. is the most popular destination for honeymooners? ....

5. A study by UNESCO once concluded that 40 percent of the world's historic and artistic assets are in which country? ....

6. In Jamaica, wedding cakes are typically made with dried fruits that have been soaked in what? ....

7. In which country might you find a heart-shaped piñata at a wedding? ....

8. What might a bride in Greece tuck into her glove to ensure a sweet life? ....
....

9. Those with a taste for extravagance can get married at Las Vegas Villa, former home of what famous flamboyant performer? ....

10. This city, one of the most popular honeymoon destinations in the U.S., is a sister city to the equally romantic Assisi, Italy; Paris, France; and Sydney, Australia.
....

11. What popular honeymoon destination straddles the U.S.-Canadian border?
....

12. In which romantic city are civil marriages performed in the Palazzo Cavalli, a 16th-century castle overlooking the Grand Canal? ....

name   *score*

Honeymoon Trivia

How much do you know about some of the most popular honeymoon destinations? You have three minutes to finish.

1. What romantic city is known as the City of Light? ....

2. What popular honeymoon destination is the largest island in French Polynesia? ....

3. In Bermuda, what is customarily placed on top of the wedding cake? ....

4. Which state in the U.S. is the most popular destination for honeymooners? ....

5. A study by UNESCO once concluded that 40 percent of the world's historic and artistic assets are in which country? ....

6. In Jamaica, wedding cakes are typically made with dried fruits that have been soaked in what? ....

7. In which country might you find a heart-shaped piñata at a wedding? ....

8. What might a bride in Greece tuck into her glove to ensure a sweet life? ....

9. Those with a taste for extravagance can get married at Las Vegas Villa, former home of what famous flamboyant performer? ....

10. This city, one of the most popular honeymoon destinations in the U.S., is a sister city to the equally romantic Assisi, Italy; Paris, France; and Sydney, Australia. ....

11. What popular honeymoon destination straddles the U.S.-Canadian border? ....

12. In which romantic city are civil marriages performed in the Palazzo Cavalli, a 16th-century castle overlooking the Grand Canal? ....

name   *score*

Honeymoon Trivia

How much do you know about some of the most popular honeymoon destinations? You have three minutes to finish.

1. What romantic city is known as the City of Light? ....

2. What popular honeymoon destination is the largest island in French Polynesia?
....

3. In Bermuda, what is customarily placed on top of the wedding cake? ....
....

4. Which state in the U.S. is the most popular destination for honeymooners? ....

5. A study by UNESCO once concluded that 40 percent of the world's historic and artistic assets are in which country? ....

6. In Jamaica, wedding cakes are typically made with dried fruits that have been soaked in what? ....

7. In which country might you find a heart-shaped piñata at a wedding? ....

8. What might a bride in Greece tuck into her glove to ensure a sweet life? ....
....

9. Those with a taste for extravagance can get married at Las Vegas Villa, former home of what famous flamboyant performer? ....

10. This city, one of the most popular honeymoon destinations in the U.S., is a sister city to the equally romantic Assisi, Italy; Paris, France; and Sydney, Australia.
....

11. What popular honeymoon destination straddles the U.S.-Canadian border?
....

12. In which romantic city are civil marriages performed in the Palazzo Cavalli, a 16th-century castle overlooking the Grand Canal? ....

name

score

Honeymoon Trivia

How much do you know about some of the most popular honeymoon destinations? You have three minutes to finish.

1. What romantic city is known as the City of Light? ....

2. What popular honeymoon destination is the largest island in French Polynesia?
    ....

3. In Bermuda, what is customarily placed on top of the wedding cake? ....
    ....

4. Which state in the U.S. is the most popular destination for honeymooners? ....

5. A study by UNESCO once concluded that 40 percent of the world's historic and artistic
    assets are in which country? ....

6. In Jamaica, wedding cakes are typically made with dried fruits that have been soaked
    in what? ....

7. In which country might you find a heart-shaped piñata at a wedding? ....

8. What might a bride in Greece tuck into her glove to ensure a sweet life? ....
    ....

9. Those with a taste for extravagance can get married at Las Vegas Villa, former home
    of what famous flamboyant performer? ....

10. This city, one of the most popular honeymoon destinations in the U.S., is a sister city
    to the equally romantic Assisi, Italy; Paris, France; and Sydney, Australia.
    ....

11. What popular honeymoon destination straddles the U.S.-Canadian border?
    ....

12. In which romantic city are civil marriages performed in the Palazzo Cavalli,
    a 16th-century castle overlooking the Grand Canal? ....

name *score*

Honeymoon Trivia

How much do you know about some of the most popular honeymoon destinations? You have three minutes to finish.

1. What romantic city is known as the City of Light? ....

2. What popular honeymoon destination is the largest island in French Polynesia?
   ....

3. In Bermuda, what is customarily placed on top of the wedding cake?....................
   ....

4. Which state in the U.S. is the most popular destination for honeymooners?.................

5. A study by UNESCO once concluded that 40 percent of the world's historic and artistic assets are in which country?...

6. In Jamaica, wedding cakes are typically made with dried fruits that have been soaked in what?..

7. In which country might you find a heart-shaped piñata at a wedding?.......................

8. What might a bride in Greece tuck into her glove to ensure a sweet life?....................
   ....

9. Those with a taste for extravagance can get married at Las Vegas Villa, former home of what famous flamboyant performer? ....

10. This city, one of the most popular honeymoon destinations in the U.S., is a sister city to the equally romantic Assisi, Italy; Paris, France; and Sydney, Australia.
    ....

11. What popular honeymoon destination straddles the U.S.-Canadian border?
    ....

12. In which romantic city are civil marriages performed in the Palazzo Cavalli, a 16th-century castle overlooking the Grand Canal?...........................

name   *score*

Honeymoon Trivia

How much do you know about some of the most popular honeymoon destinations? You have three minutes to finish.

1. What romantic city is known as the City of Light? ....

2. What popular honeymoon destination is the largest island in French Polynesia?
....

3. In Bermuda, what is customarily placed on top of the wedding cake? ....
....

4. Which state in the U.S. is the most popular destination for honeymooners? ....

5. A study by UNESCO once concluded that 40 percent of the world's historic and artistic assets are in which country? ....

6. In Jamaica, wedding cakes are typically made with dried fruits that have been soaked in what? ....

7. In which country might you find a heart-shaped piñata at a wedding? ....

8. What might a bride in Greece tuck into her glove to ensure a sweet life? ....
....

9. Those with a taste for extravagance can get married at Las Vegas Villa, former home of what famous flamboyant performer? ....

10. This city, one of the most popular honeymoon destinations in the U.S., is a sister city to the equally romantic Assisi, Italy; Paris, France; and Sydney, Australia.
....

11. What popular honeymoon destination straddles the U.S.-Canadian border?
....

12. In which romantic city are civil marriages performed in the Palazzo Cavalli, a 16th-century castle overlooking the Grand Canal? ....

name *score*

Honeymoon Trivia

How much do you know about some of the most popular honeymoon destinations? You have three minutes to finish.

1. What romantic city is known as the City of Light? ....

2. What popular honeymoon destination is the largest island in French Polynesia? ....

3. In Bermuda, what is customarily placed on top of the wedding cake?........................ ....

4. Which state in the U.S. is the most popular destination for honeymooners?.................

5. A study by UNESCO once concluded that 40 percent of the world's historic and artistic assets are in which country?...

6. In Jamaica, wedding cakes are typically made with dried fruits that have been soaked in what? ....

7. In which country might you find a heart-shaped piñata at a wedding?........................

8. What might a bride in Greece tuck into her glove to ensure a sweet life?.................... ....

9. Those with a taste for extravagance can get married at Las Vegas Villa, former home of what famous flamboyant performer? ....

10. This city, one of the most popular honeymoon destinations in the U.S., is a sister city to the equally romantic Assisi, Italy; Paris, France; and Sydney, Australia. ....

11. What popular honeymoon destination straddles the U.S.-Canadian border? ....

12. In which romantic city are civil marriages performed in the Palazzo Cavalli, a 16th-century castle overlooking the Grand Canal?.................................

name   *score*

Honeymoon Trivia

How much do you know about some of the most popular honeymoon destinations? You have three minutes to finish.

1. What romantic city is known as the City of Light? ....

2. What popular honeymoon destination is the largest island in French Polynesia? ....

3. In Bermuda, what is customarily placed on top of the wedding cake? ....

4. Which state in the U.S. is the most popular destination for honeymooners? ....

5. A study by UNESCO once concluded that 40 percent of the world's historic and artistic assets are in which country? ....

6. In Jamaica, wedding cakes are typically made with dried fruits that have been soaked in what? ....

7. In which country might you find a heart-shaped piñata at a wedding? ....

8. What might a bride in Greece tuck into her glove to ensure a sweet life? ....

9. Those with a taste for extravagance can get married at Las Vegas Villa, former home of what famous flamboyant performer? ....

10. This city, one of the most popular honeymoon destinations in the U.S., is a sister city to the equally romantic Assisi, Italy; Paris, France; and Sydney, Australia. ....

11. What popular honeymoon destination straddles the U.S.-Canadian border? ....

12. In which romantic city are civil marriages performed in the Palazzo Cavalli, a 16th-century castle overlooking the Grand Canal? ....

name *score*

Honeymoon Trivia

How much do you know about some of the most popular honeymoon destinations? You have three minutes to finish.

1. What romantic city is known as the City of Light? ....

2. What popular honeymoon destination is the largest island in French Polynesia?
....

3. In Bermuda, what is customarily placed on top of the wedding cake?.....................
....

4. Which state in the U.S. is the most popular destination for honeymooners?................

5. A study by UNESCO once concluded that 40 percent of the world's historic and artistic assets are in which country?...

6. In Jamaica, wedding cakes are typically made with dried fruits that have been soaked in what?...

7. In which country might you find a heart-shaped piñata at a wedding?.......................

8. What might a bride in Greece tuck into her glove to ensure a sweet life?...................
....

9. Those with a taste for extravagance can get married at Las Vegas Villa, former home of what famous flamboyant performer? ....

10. This city, one of the most popular honeymoon destinations in the U.S., is a sister city to the equally romantic Assisi, Italy; Paris, France; and Sydney, Australia.
....

11. What popular honeymoon destination straddles the U.S.-Canadian border?
....

12. In which romantic city are civil marriages performed in the Palazzo Cavalli, a 16th-century castle overlooking the Grand Canal?...

name   *score*

Gift Registry

from	gift	Thank-you sent
....	....	⬤
....	....	⬤
....	....	⬤
....	....	⬤
....	....	⬤
....	....	⬤
....	....	⬤
....	....	⬤
....	....	⬤
....	....	⬤
....	....	⬤

Gift Registry

from	gift	Thank-you sent
		◯
		◯
		◯
		◯
		◯
		◯
		◯
		◯
		◯
		◯